Content

American Dream Horses

The earliest ancestors of the horse lived in America about 50 million years ago. They did not look much like horses, they only measured three hands and had four toes. Over time the species developed and began to look more like the horses we recognize. About 10,000 years ago, during the Ice Age, the species died out in America and the continent was without horses for a long time.

In the 15th century, the horse made a comeback thanks to Christopher Columbus and the Spanish Conquistadors who brought horses with them when they went ashore the Caribbean Islands in 1493.

Today there are many breeds, types and colors of horses in America. It's hard to define what the difference is between a breed and a type, because not everyone agrees on this subject. Horses of one breed can be registered with another, and new breeds are being created due to the crossbreeding of already existing breeds. Some people say you don't get a new breed this way, only a crossbred horse. Examples of this are the AraAppaloosa (Arabian + Appaloosa),

Cremello
The skin is pinkish, the eyes are blue, the coat is creamy white, and the manes and tail are white.

Perlino
The skin is pinkish, the eyes are blue, the coat is white or cream and the manes and tail are darker, either rust or orange-hued.

Buckskin
The coat is golden, from pale cream to dark copper, and the manes and tail are black or dark brown.

the Walkaloosa (Tennessee Walking Horse + Appaloosa) and the Quarab (Quarter + Arabian). There are different color registers, in which horses of different breeds have been entered. The most famous are the Palomino and the Pinto, but there are many more, like the Buckskin, Cremello and Perlino. There are also height registers, in which horses are entered by height, and registers for horses of a special type or with special gaits.

There are American horses in all colors and patterns, and there will surely be equine colors you have never heard of. Here are a few colors that are less well known:

Smoky cream
The skin is pinkish, the eyes are blue, the coat, manes and tail are light, with a copper hue.

Grulla (pronounced: grew-yah)
The coat is light to brownish blue-gray, with black primitive markings and dorsal stripes. Grulla is the rarest equine color. The word *grulla* is Spanish and means "crane".

Mustang

Hernando Cortez brought horses ashore in Mexico in 1519, and later other Spanish Conquistadors, adventurers and missionaries followed with their horses. These were strong, healthy Spanish horses, mostly crossbreeds between Andalusians, Arabians, Barbs and Jennet horses. The name Mustang comes from the Spanish word *mesteño*, which means wild or stray. The horses survived the harsh trip across the sea, which is a testament to their stamina. Afterwards, they spread over North America and the Native Americans didn't have much of a defense from the gun-carrying newcomers on their horses.

Ultimately, the Native Americans became very adept at stealing the settlers' horses. In the beginning, the animals were eaten or set free, but the Native Americans soon realized that they were valuable riding animals. Spotted horses were especially popular, probably because of their natural camouflage colors. The Native Americans eventually became real horse experts, and some tribes even started actual horse breeding farms.

The horses that were set free or fled, lived in herds in the wild. In the mid-19th century, there were more than two million wild horses in America, but by the end of the century this number had decreased. Farms and possessions had spread over the country, and the territory that was available for wild horses had rapidly shrunk. At the same time, many wild horses were killed: they were a threat to farmers because they ate the harvest, and in addition they provided cheap meat for the animal feed industry.

Today, the Mustang is a protected animal. There are only about 50,000 left and many herds are so small that they suffer from inbreeding.

▼ Description

Wild horses are only fully grown when they are 4 to 7 years old. In spring and summer they grow at a normal rate but, during fall and winter, they hardly grow at all because they do not have much food.

During cold weather they need all their energy to keep their bodies warm. Their exterior varies and often reveals which bloodlines are dominant. Some herds have characteristics of the Quarter, others look more like other breeds, for example the Thoroughbred, Arabian or Morgan. Also, the colors differ; some herds have mainly spotted horses, while others mostly have bay horses. Wild horses have strong legs which are stronger than those of other horses. The hooves are stronger than average because they have to be able to run without shoes on any kind of terrain.

▼ Use

It is obvious that you can't really "use" a wild horse, but Mustangs can be tamed. If tame, they can be used as saddle horses.

▼ The herd

Each herd has two leaders: a mare and a stallion. The mare leads the herd. When the herd is galloping, the stallion is usually at the back to check that all horses are coming along and keeping up with the pace. The stallion protects the herd when there is danger; he will go to the front, ready to challenge any intruder. He is constantly on guard, so the rest of the herd can graze and rest. Young stallions are chased away from the herd when they are two or three years old and the young mares are in season for the first time.

These young animals form their own herds. This is the way nature fights inbreeding.

Kiger Mustang

The Mustang of today does not look like the Spanish horses from which it descends, but in 1977 a herd of Mustangs was discovered that strongly deviated from other herds. These horses were light yellow and had dorsal and zebra stripes on their legs. Furthermore, they had the head of a Barb. The Mustangs, which were found in Oregon, lived closed off from other herds, so they were able to keep their original characteristics. The herd was split into two groups: 20 horses in one and seven in the other. The herds were set free and supervised to make sure no other wild horses would come near them and breed with these Kiger Mustangs.

A few Kiger Mustangs were tamed. They turned out to be good learners and were well suited for cattle driving.

Height
Generally, the height varies from 13.2 to 15 hands. The leaders are usually taller than the other horses in the herd.

Colors
Mustangs come in all possible equine colors, but most are sorrel.

Cayuse Indian Pony

The pioneers often called the horses of the Native Americans "Cayuse ponies", but the Cayuse Indian Pony is, in fact, a breed that can be traced back to the 19th century. Their background and exterior clearly differs from the Mustang, Barb and other wild horses. Like many other horse breeds, the Cayuse Indian Pony has a somewhat fuzzy history, but it is believed to be a descendant of French horses, that came to Canada in the seventeenth century.

The Canadians mostly used the Percheron to improve their own horse breeds, which was not a bad choice because the Percheron is one of few work horses that can trot over long distances. Many years later, the Canadians took their horses to America and the Native Americans (who were masters in stealing horses) crossbred them with Spanish horses in order to breed a lively horse with good stamina. Around 1800, the Cayuse Indian Pony had become a breed of its own. It was known everywhere that the Cayuse Native Americans in the Northwest could handle horses very well; they bred horses efficiently and selectively and, because French horses were spotted, the Native Americans ended up with very colorful horses. At present, the breed is rarely found outside the state of California. The American Wild Horse Research Center has created a registry of wild horses and ponies with Barb blood, among which is the Cayuse Indian Pony.

▼ Description

The Cayuse Indian Pony is small and stocky, with high withers and extremely long cannon bones.

▼ Use

The pony is mostly used for riding and is a great animal for children because it rides easily and comfortably.

Colors
Mostly gray.

Height
Usually about
14 hands.

Florida Cracker Horse

Colors
The horses have all possible equine colors but are mostly solid or gray.

The Florida Cracker Horse is another rare breed. It is also called the Florida Horse, Woods Pony, Marsh Tacky, Seminole Pony, Indian Pony, Prairie Pony or Florida Cow Pony. There are many breeds in its pedigree, among which are the Arabian, Barb, Andalusian, Sorraia and the Spanish Jennet horse. From the exterior it looks a lot like the Mustang, but it also has some characteristics of the Criollo, the Peruvian Paso and the Paso Fino. The breed was created by natural selection among the herds of wild horses in Florida, and it became a favorite as a cattle driver on the farm. Later however, farmers started using bigger horses for this task, almost causing the extinction of the Florida Cracker Horse. The breed was named after one of the tools the Spanish cowboys used to drive cattle, a "cracker". This is a long whip that they let sound in the air.

▼ Description

The Florida Cracker Horse is a small horse. It has an elegant head with lively eyes, the back is short and strong with rounded loins. The horse has a natural alertness, power and stamina. It is born with a fast gait. Many horses of this breed have a natural gait called the "coon rack".

▼ Use

The Florida Cracker Horse is used for recreational riding.

Height
13.5 to 15 hands.

American Quarter Horse

Nobody can tell with certainty how the Quarterhorse was created. Some people claim that it is the oldest horse breed in the United States, and is based on the Chickasaw horses that were secured from the Native Americans. These were small, stocky horses, probably of Spanish origin. The pioneers were interested in competitions and naturally they wanted very fast horses. It is assumed that the Thoroughbred horses, that came to the United States before the studbook had been created in England, were used for breeding Quarters.

The Quarterhorse was named after the distance of the competitions, the quarter mile. All over the U.S. many competitions were organized, but not on the nice race tracks we know today. Most of the time they were held on some open land or an open space.

The competitions were between horse owners or the riders, and the competition was won by whoever had the fastest horse. The breeding of Quarters and Thoroughbreds in the U.S. happened at the same pace. Some Thoroughbreds were used as studs for both breeds and many short-distance horses were registered as Thoroughbreds in the American studbook, even though not all their bloodlines could be traced back to the English studbook. Another theory is that the Quarterhorse was bred in the Southwest much later.

There, people mainly held short-distance competitions and the cowboys needed a horse that could accelerate very fast, could be ridden easily, and was suitable to work with cattle.

Maybe it would have been better if they had called the Quarters of that time, a horse "type" instead of a "breed", but today the Quarterhorse is definitely considered a breed of its own.

▼ Description

The head is short and broad in comparison to the small pricked ears, the hindquarters are strong and muscled. The bow is powerful which gives the saddle a good base. The back is exceptionally short. The Quarterhorse has a nice disposition, is intelligent and a fast learner.

The American Quarter Horse Association, founded in 1940, is the largest breed organization in the world. It has almost four million members!

▼ Use

Most people think of Western riding when talking about Quarterhorses, but this horse is also a competition horse. It has become increasingly popular in disciplines such as polo and jumping. It is also an outstanding recreational horse.

The Quarterhorse is named after the distance of the competitions in which it ran, the quarter mile. The horse was first called Quarter-pather, later "Colonial quarter of a mile running horse (!)", and finally American Quarterhorse.

Quarter + Arabian = Quarab

In 1989, a register was created for the crossbreeds between Arabians and Quarters, and in 1991 another register was created in which the Paint was allowed. A Quarab can only have Arabian, Quarter or Paint blood, and both its parents have to be registered in their breed register. The Quarab looks like an Arabian or a Quarterhorse. The head is mostly elegant with big eyes, a broad forehead and a concave nose. The height varies from 14 to 16 hands.

Colors

All solid colors are allowed, and the horse can have markings on legs and head. If there is too much white it will be registered as a Painthorse.

Height
Average 15.2 hands.

American Saddlebred

The American Saddlebred has its origins in the 17th century, when British pioneers brought their Galloway and recreational horses to North America. These horse breeds were both small and strong, and very suitable for riding on rough terrain. Eventually, the Narraganset Pacer breed was developed, but when the pioneers settled, they had only this sturdy breed. Roads were constructed and the demand for good riding horses increased. To breed a lighter riding horse, the Narraganset Pacer was crossbred with the English Thoroughbred in the 18th century. This way, a versatile riding horse was created that was considered a stable breed in 1776. The breeders called the horse the American Horse.

The Thoroughbred stallion that had the most influence on the American Horse was Messenger. He was a gray of 15.3 hands. He had good trot characteristics, which he passed on to the American Saddlebred, and is also seen as the foundation sire of the trotting horse breed the American Standardbred.

In Kentucky, riding horses were bred on a large scale during the 19th century, and mid-19th century, the American Saddlebred breed was created. However, it would be wrong to say that the American Saddlebred comes from Kentucky, because horses from the neighboring states of Tennessee, Illinois, Iowa, Indiana and Ohio have also contributed to the creation of the breed. Missouri was a rival of Kentucky when it came to horses, and most people from Missouri strongly maintain that, despite claims to the contrary, they have bred the very best riding horses.

Two stallions are considered the foundation sires of the Saddlebred: Gaines Denmark and Harrison Chief. About 60 percent of all Saddlebreds are descendants of Gaines Denmark. Gaines Denmark and Harrison Chief both came eight generations after the Thoroughbred Blaze. The breed has become extremely popular because of its good characteristics as a riding horse, and at the end of the 19th century their breeders wanted to find a breed association. In April, 1891 they called a meeting in Kentucky and, that same day, the association was founded. It was the very first horse breed association in the United States.

▼ Description

A good American Saddlebred should have a harmonious conformation, good muscles and a soft glowing coat. The mares should be "feminine", and the stallions real machos. The head should be beautifully shaped with big expressive eyes, ears that are close to one another, a straight nose and large nostrils. You should be able to distinguish a Saddlebred from a Quarter just by looking at the head.

▼ Gaits

In addition to the walk, trot and canter, the Saddlebred has the following gaits:

Animated walk
The "Animated walk" is a diagonal gait in two tempi, with the same foot fall as the trot. It looks like a bouncy, collected walk.

Slow gait
The "Slow gait" is a collected gait in four tempi. The legs are moved as with the walk but the horse keeps each leg up in the air for a moment when it is lifted.

Rocking horse canter
The collected short canter – looks as if the horse is going up and down like a rocking horse.

▼ Use

The American Saddlebred is, as the name suggests, a riding horse. It is very well suited for dressage, jumping, terrain riding and Western riding, but it is also used in carriage driving.

 It is claimed that if a Saddlebred is good at this gait, it can canter a whole day in the shade of a tree!

Height
14.2 to 17.2 hands.

Colors
All colors are permitted, but the most common are sorrel, brown and black, as well as gray, palomino and mixes.

23

Appaloosa

The Appaloosa is an ancient breed. Cave paintings of more than 20,000 years ago display these spotted horses, and the old Chinese emperors called them "celestial horses". In the 18th and 19th century, they were favored by the European artistocracy. In the United States the breed is all about the Native Americans, especially the Nez Perce tribe which lived in Oregon. It was the only Native American tribe that bred horses efficiently and selectively, and the Nez Perce were known as real horse experts. Only the best stallions were used for breeding; the others were gelded, so they could not have any descendants.

The Nez Perce were also very handy. The horses which did not qualify were traded with other Native American tribes. The horses of the Nez Perce eventually grew to be strong, fast animals which had strong legs and could be used on rough terrain, which was precisely what the Native Americans wanted. The spotted horses were the most popular. The Native Americans called the spotted horse "paulouse", after the Paulouse river which ran through the landscape where the horses of the Nez Perce grazed. Later the word "Paulouse" became Appaloosa in everyday speech.

Unfortunately, the Nez Perce Native did not have a pleasant fate, which had consequences for the Appaloosa breed. The Native Americans fell from favor with the authorities, and were chased off to Canada. They did not make it farther than Montana, where they surrendered. The Appaloosa horses, the strength and pride of the Native Americans, were confiscated by the army and sold. There was even a bounty on the killing of escaped Appaloosas! The beautiful Appaloosa stallions of the Native Americans were gone and all they had left were powerful pulling horses. The breed had to cope with this for generations, but at present the Appaloosa is a lighter type: a result of crossbreeding with the English Thoroughbred and the Quarter.

For fifty years the Appaloosa

was a rare breed, but in 1938 the Appaloosa Horse Club was founded with the goal of saving the breed.

▼ Description

The Appaloosa of today has many characteristics that the Nez Perce greatly appreciated: stamina, good character and versatility. The horse has a body with strong hindquarters, good legs and hard hooves. The head is elegant.

▼ Use

There are different Appaloosa bloodlines. Some are characterized by speed, others are very suited for Western disciplines like cutting and roping, while others are good for dressage and jumping. You could almost say there is an Appaloosa for every use.

Height
Most Appaloosas are between 14.2 to 15.2 hands, and are therefore considered small horses.

▼ Colors

The breed distinguishes itself from all other breeds by the special Appaloosa pattern. The most common pattern is a dark body with a spotted or white coat on the loins and hind-quarters. However, there are several patterns – from "snowflake" (dark body with lighter spots and markings) to "leopard" (white body with black spots everywhere). No two Appaloosas are the same, but they have three characteristics in common: 1. a spotted coat (especially around the muzzle, eyes and genitalia), 2. striped hooves, and 3. a white sclera (ring) around the iris, just like human eyes.

Appaloosa + Arabian = AraAppaloosa!

The AraAppaloosa is actually not a new horse breed, even though it recently received its own breed association. The AraAppaloosa and Foundation Breeder's International (AAFBI) is a foundation for breeders who crossbreed Appaloosas with Arabians to arrive at, what is to them, the original Appaloosa. The spotted horse is considered one of the oldest horse breeds in the world, and some people believe it was originally an Arabian. The Arabian is a very old breed, according to stories from Egypt and the Middle East, it was often spotted. Claude Thompson, who was the founder of the Appaloosa Horse Club in 1938, had seen the Appaloosas of the Nez Perce during his childhood, and he was convinced that crossbreeding with Arabian blood was the only way to bring back the original breed. At the time the Arabian was the only breed that could be crossbred with the Appaloosa, so the breed had had Arabian blood for a long time.

The AraAppaloosa is definitely a beautiful horse that combines the colors and the good character of the Appaloosa with the elegance, health and the stamina of the Arabian.

Morgan

The Morgan is named after Justin Morgan, a teacher from Massachusetts. When Morgan moved to Vermont in 1789 he brought a bay foal with him. The young stallion was named Figure, and is considered the foundation sire of the Morgan breed. Nobody knew for sure which breed Figure was, but he probably had Arabian or Thoroughbred blood. When Justin Morgan died, Figure was called the Justin Morgan horse. The small stallion (Figure only measured 14 hands) became a celebrity in New England – not just because of his beauty but also because of his fantastic disposition, stamina, power and speed. He became a popular stud because all of these good characteristics were passed on to his descendants.

Most of Figure's life was spent as a working horse on farms, but he also participated in competitions. He died in 1821 of injuries he received when another horse kicked him. Three of his descendants, the stallions Sherman, Bulrush and Woodbury, all passed on Figure's good characteristics to the next generations of Morgans.

The first Morgans were used for the clearing of forests and plowing of fields, but in New England they also served well as carriage horses.

During the years following 1840, a few breeders started to bring unity to the breeding of Morgans. They found second, third and fourth generation descendants of Figure and made them the foundations of the breed. The Morgan became a popular and expensive breed, which was sold all over the U.S.

At the very early start of trotting races the Morgan was one of the most popular breeds, but the horse is still considered mainly a work horse or an all-rounder. During the Civil War, many Morgans were used in the Cavalry. Unfortunately, many of them died during the battles.

Nowadays, you can find Morgans all over the U.S., as well as in more than 20 countries outside the U.S.

Colors

Bay, black, chestnut, yellow, light gray or yellow, cream and buckskin. There are even registered Morgans with an overo pattern. The most common colors are bay, black and chestnut.

Height

14.1 to 15.2 hands.

▼ Description

The Morgan has stamina, is honest and easy-going and moves well and freely. The head should be short and expressive with a broad forehead, large eyes and a straight or somewhat concave bridge of the nose. The ears are short and well-formed and are far apart. The mares' ears are somewhat longer than those of the stallion. The body is compact, with a short back (weak, low or long backs are considered serious defaults in a Morgan), broad loins and a deep flank. It has a high attached tail, which is worn graciously. The Morgan's loins can never be higher than its withers.

▼ Use

The Morgan is a popular riding horse, but it is also used for carriage driving, Western riding, jumping, dressage and endurance.

Because of its calm character the horse is sometimes used for therapy. Everyone who has bought a Morgan says it is not just a new horse, but a new member of the family – that's how friendly and nice the horse is!

Morgan + Arabian = Morab

Some people think that a Morab is just partbred Morgan and Arabian, but in fact it is its own breed, even though it has Morgan and Arabian blood. Only the first generation Morabs are half Arabian and half Morgan. In addition there are Morabs which were bred from Morabs and a breed was created.

American Paint Horse

The Spanish adventurer Hernando Cortes sailed to America in 1519, chasing gold. He had 16 horses with him on his journey. One of these horses was a chestnut horse with white spots on its belly – this horse that, together with the Mustangs, was the basis for the Paint breed.

Many, many years later, in 1960, Rebecca Tyler Lockhart was sitting at her kitchen table calling her acquaintances. She had an idea. Many people had been interested in spotted ranch horses, and now Rebecca wanted to register all of these horses and make them part of a breed association. Many people thought it was a good idea, and Rebecca put everything on paper. Eventually her whole kitchen table was covered with little notes, and she had to call two friends to help her keep track of everything. It went fine, until all three of them got the flu. Rebecca had to call three more friends for help.

They received the help, and the team was able to found an open class for spotted horses during a horse event in Fort Worth in 1961. The friends called everyone they knew who owned Paint horses; just the word "competition" was enough to entice people. A few weeks after the event, Rebecca held a meeting with seventeen other people to discuss if they could found a breed.

In 1962, Rebecca was once again sitting at her kitchen table, but now she was able to register the very first Paint horse with the American Paint Stock Horse Association. It was a black stallion with white tobiano colors called Bandits Pinto. Before the year had ended, she had 150 members and 250 registered horses.

Since then, the breed has only become more widespread – at present the breed association has more than half a million registered Paint horses. The breed is spread all over the world, but wherever the horses are born, they are included in the American register, which is now called American Paint Horse Association.

▼ Description

The Painthorse is compact and muscular, with a relatively small head. It has an exceptionally good character. Because of its conformation, it is fast and can make rounds on the spot. This is why it is very suitable for Western riding. It is said to have a kind of "cow sense".

▼ Use

The Paint is mostly used for riding and it is suitable for all disciplines in Western riding.

Overo is a Spanish word, which means "as an egg". In the United States overo usually just means "paint, but no tobiano!"

Cannot be bred easily

When breeding other horse breeds, attention is paid to conformation and character, less to color. This is unfortunate for the Painthorse breeders, because not only do they have to concentrate on good conformation and character, they also need to create the desired colors and patterns!

Height
14.5 to 16.5 hands.

Colors

The three main colors are called tobiano, overo and tovero, but within overo there are different patterns: framed overo, sabino and splashed white. The spots can be all equine colors – they are therefore called pied.

▼ Tobiano

A horse with a tobiano pattern has color on one or both flanks, while all of its legs are usually white over the knees. The spots are equal and clear, oval or round and stretch from the neck to the breast, like a shield. The head is pinto, and the markings are solid colors with blaze, star, spots, etc. The tail is often two-colored, and a tobiano is either mostly white or mostly pied.

▼ Tovero

The tovero is pied around the ears, muzzle and often also on its forehead up to the eyes. It has one or two blue eyes, spots on its breast and sometimes on its neck. The spots are different in size, often the spots on its belly and towards the loins are smaller. The horse can have spots of different sizes at the croup.

▼ Overo

A horse with an overo pattern does not usually have white on its back between the withers and tail, and one or more legs may be pied. The white spots are irregular, as if someone has splattered white paint over it. The horse has a lot of white in the face and the tail is usually one color. The overo is mostly white or mostly pied just like the tobiano.

Frame overo – The horse has a lot of white on the head and white spots on its flank and neck. Seen from the side, it is as if it is white with a pied frame. The legs are usually pied, sometimes with white socks. Both eyes are blue.

Sabino (also called calico overo) – White on legs and head, usually white spots on its belly. The pied coat can be gray and its eyes brown or blue. Some sabinos are almost completely white, with only a little color on their ears!

Splashed white – White legs and belly and a lot of white on the head. The white spots are in clear contrast with the pied parts, as if the horse has been dipped in white paint. The eyes are often blue. This is the rarest overo color, but it is becoming increasingly popular among breeders.

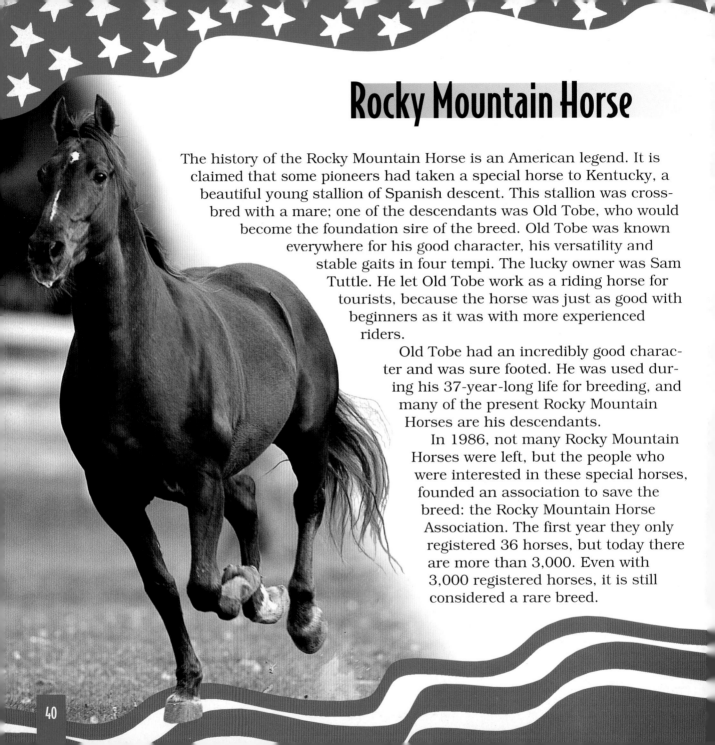

Rocky Mountain Horse

The history of the Rocky Mountain Horse is an American legend. It is claimed that some pioneers had taken a special horse to Kentucky, a beautiful young stallion of Spanish descent. This stallion was cross-bred with a mare; one of the descendants was Old Tobe, who would become the foundation sire of the breed. Old Tobe was known everywhere for his good character, his versatility and stable gaits in four tempi. The lucky owner was Sam Tuttle. He let Old Tobe work as a riding horse for tourists, because the horse was just as good with beginners as it was with more experienced riders.

Old Tobe had an incredibly good character and was sure footed. He was used during his 37-year-long life for breeding, and many of the present Rocky Mountain Horses are his descendants.

In 1986, not many Rocky Mountain Horses were left, but the people who were interested in these special horses, founded an association to save the breed: the Rocky Mountain Horse Association. The first year they only registered 36 horses, but today there are more than 3,000. Even with 3,000 registered horses, it is still considered a rare breed.

▼ Description

Breeding is meticulously inspected and only horses with the right characteristics are registered. They should have good character, natural gaits, a broad breast and sloping chest (45°). The Rocky Mountain Horses are easy to deal with and sure footed. They are usually calm and intelligent.

▼ Use

The Rocky Mountain Horse is used for hobbies, riding, competitions and endurance.

Colors

All solid colors are allowed. They cannot have white above the knees, and can only have modest white markings on their face. A great number of horses are chocolate brown with almost white manes and tail, but there are also many sorrel, bay and black horses.

Height
14.2 to 16 hands.

Tennessee Walking Horse

Large plantations were created in the 19th century, and the farmers needed horses that could walk through the crops without destroying everything. The plantations were so big that the people who worked there needed to sit in the saddle for hours at a time. Therefore, the horse also had to be comfortable to sit on. To breed a horse that lived up to these desires, the breeders used the Narraganset Pacer, the Canadian Pacer, the Thoroughbred, the Morgan, the Saddlebred and the Standardbred (an American trotting horse).

The horse that influenced the breed the most was named Black Allan. He was a crossbreed between a Standardbred and a Morgan, born in 1886. Black Allan was supposed to become a trotting horse, but that didn't work out because he couldn't trot! He did have a peculiar way of walking, which turned out to be very comfortable for the rider. He passed on this gait to all of his descendants.

In 1914 another stallion came into the picture, who was called Giovanni. Giovanni had Saddlebred blood, and after he became involved in the breeding process, the breed became nobler. And it still is noble.

In 1935, a breed association was founded for the Tennessee Walking Horse. The first year, 208 horses were registered, but at the end of the century more than 350,000 were registered!

▼ Description

The head is beautiful with small ears. The shoulders are long and sloped, the back is very short and strong. The horse carries its head high and makes long steps. It is a fast learner but also has a fiery temperament, so it is not really a horse for beginners.

▼ Use

The Tennessee Walking Horse is used for riding, with or without a carriage. It is very suitable for endurance, because of its fun gait. It is also used for Western riding and lately also for dressage, although its trot is not very good.

Height
Average
15.2 hands.

Colors
The Tennessee Walking Horse exists in all equine colors, even spotted.

▼ Gaits

The Tennessee Walking Horse has three gaits: flat walk, running walk and rocking chair canter.

Flat walk

This is a pleasant gait in four tempi with each of the horse's feet hitting the ground separately at regular intervals. The speed is about four to eight miles an hour. The hind leg hits the ground before the foreleg is lifted, and the head will nod in rhythm with the cadence of the movements. This last characteristic is true for all horses, but it is very pronounced with the Tennessee Walking Horse.

Running walk

This is a very supple, gliding gait for which the Tennessee Walking Horse is especially known. This gait resembles the flat walk, but the speed is higher. At high speed, the horse over-steps the front track with the back foot by a distance of six to 18 inches. The more "stride" the horse has, the better a "walker" it is considered to be. Even though it can go as fast as 10 to 20 miles an hour, this is a very relaxed gait for the horse. Some muscles can be completely relaxed, which makes the horses flop their ears in rhythm or even snap their teeth.

Rocking horse canter

This is a collected short canter, just like the regular canter, but as the name may depict, the Tennessee Walking Horse has an extra smooth and relaxed canter, which is very comfortable for the rider.

Missouri Fox Trotting Horse

The pioneers in Missouri, Kentucky, Illinois, Tennessee and Arkansas needed horses that they could use for work on the farm, in the forest or with their cattle. It was important that the animals were sure-footed, because large parts of these states are mountainous. Over time, the pioneers developed a horse that was suitable for all of these tasks, the Missouri Fox Trotter.

It had an incredibly nice character and a special flowing gait in four tempi. In 1948 a breed association was founded; in 1958 it was reorganized, and it was called the Missouri Fox Trotting Horse Breed Association. The breeders have done their utmost to improve the horse until it became the versatile recreational and instructional horse of today. It is still sure-footed on rough terrain, and thanks to its supple walk, it is a pleasure to ride for long distances. There is a Fox Trotter for every use: an excellent work horse for farmers, a sure-footed horse with stamina for hunters and rangers, and an intelligent, calm horse for the film industry in Hollywood.

The breed has three natural gaits: a supple, long gait which is called the "flat-foot walk", a fun calm "foxtrot" and a rocking horse-like short canter which is called the "rocking horse canter". These gaits are natural to the horse; they are neither taught nor stimulated.

▼ Description

The Missouri Fox Trotter should have great conformation, and be able to carry a heavy load. The neck should be gracious and proportional to the length of the body. The back should be short and strong, the shoulders properly sloped and muscular. The coat should be silky and the head should radiate intelligence and alertness.

Colors
The Missouri Fox Trotter exists in all equine colors, but chestnut is the most common.

Height
14 to 16 hands.

▼ Use

Because the Fox Trotter is a comfortable riding horse, it is only logical that it is a favorite for trail rides and endurance. Ninety percent of Missouri Fox Trotters are used for trail rides, competitions and endurance.

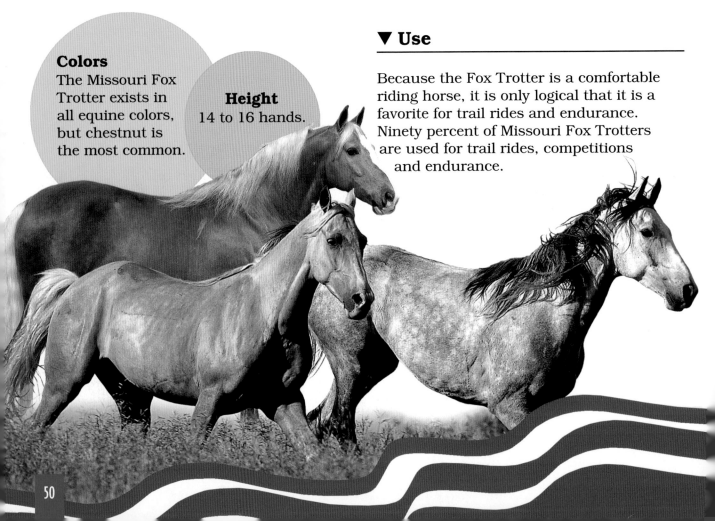

▼ Gaits

The most characteristic to this horse is the foxtrot:

Fox Trot

The foxtrot is a diagonal gait, during which the horse walks with its forelegs and trots with its hind legs. The steps are long. The legs are not lifted very high, but the horse is incredibly sure-footed, and the flowing movement to the hind leg doesn't force the rider from the saddle constantly, as when trotting. It is a very nice gait for longer distances. The horse holds its head relatively high, so it looks very elegant. The head moves a little bit with the rhythmic foot fall, which makes the horse look very relaxed and worthy.

Colorado Ranger Horse

The Colorado Ranger comes from Colorado, as the name suggests. It looks like an Appaloosa, but is not. It has its own background and history and is a separate breed. Because of the many similarities, some Rangers have incorrectly been registered as Appaloosas.

The breed was developed as a horse that could handle cattle very well, and the man who made it all happen is Mike Ruby. He kept meticulous records of all offspring that were born on his farm. He wrote down foaling dates, coat patterns and complete pedigrees. These handwritten ledgers are still with the breed association.

If you want to register a horse as a Colorado Ranger, the bloodlines have to trace back directly to the foundation sires of the breed: Patches and/or Max. Patches was a descendant of the horses General Ulysses S. Grant received from sultan Abdul Hamid of Turkey: the Arabian Leopard and the Barb Linden Tree.

Ruby founded the Colorado Ranger Horse Association in 1935, and was the president until his death. He died unexpectedly while he was outside, gathering his beloved horses.

The association, however, did not die with him, it still exists and the Colorado Rangers can still be traced back to Patches and Max.

Colors
Usually Appaloosa coloration.

Height
14.2 to 16 hands.

▼ Description

The head is intelligent, the body compact with strong legs and well-formed, hard hooves. The hindquarters are powerful.

▼ Use

The breed is used for riding.

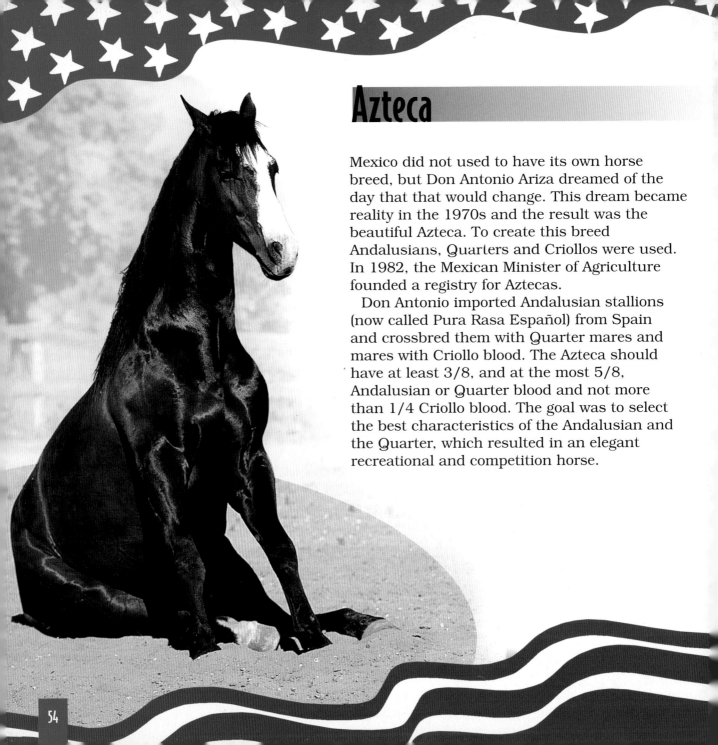

Azteca

Mexico did not used to have its own horse breed, but Don Antonio Ariza dreamed of the day that that would change. This dream became reality in the 1970s and the result was the beautiful Azteca. To create this breed Andalusians, Quarters and Criollos were used. In 1982, the Mexican Minister of Agriculture founded a registry for Aztecas.

Don Antonio imported Andalusian stallions (now called Pura Rasa Español) from Spain and crossbred them with Quarter mares and mares with Criollo blood. The Azteca should have at least 3/8, and at the most 5/8, Andalusian or Quarter blood and not more than 1/4 Criollo blood. The goal was to select the best characteristics of the Andalusian and the Quarter, which resulted in an elegant recreational and competition horse.

▼ Description

The mares' heads are medium size, the stallions' are somewhat more powerful. The back of the nose is straight and slightly convex. The eyes are expressive and lively, the manes beautiful and proud. The back is very short, straight and strong. The hindquarters are powerful, muscular and nicely arched. The legs are muscular and have strong joints. The coat should be silky.

▼ Use

The Azteca has gracious gaits, and because it is easy to ride, it is well suited for dressage. Aztecas are also used a lot in Western disciplines, while some horses are very good at jumping.

Colors

All colors are allowed, but spotted horses (with Paint or Appaloosa patterns) and albinos are excluded.

Height

Height is important for Aztecas. A full-grown mare should be between 14.1 to 15.2 hands, and a grown stallion between 14. 2 to 15.3 hands.

▼ The American Azteca Horse

A breed association for the Azteca, The American Azteca Horse, was recently founded in the United States. The distinction was made because they wanted to breed a horse with slightly different characteristics than the Mexican Azteca. This was not because they wanted to offend the Mexicans, who had created the breed, but simply because they felt that the American market was different from the Mexican market. The basis for the breeding process is still the Andalusian and the Quarter, but the breed cannot have more than 3/4 of Andalusian or Quarter blood. The height of the horse is 14.1 to 16.1 hands. All equine colors and markings are allowed.

Bashkir Curly Horse

The history of this breed is known as of 1898. One day, a boy named Peter Damele and his father were out riding when they discovered three very strange wild horses. This took place in Nevada, near a town named Austin. Father and son were both surprised, because they had never seen horses with a curly coat before and had no idea where they came from. They never found out, but they were able to catch the horses. By doing so, they formed the basis of what would later be an independent breed: the American Bashkir Curly.

In 1971, a breed register was founded to protect the breed from extinction. Owners of the Bashkir Curly were asked to register all of their horses' characteristics and, in doing so, they ultimately came to decide what the horse's characteristic traits were. A funny characteristic is that these horses lose their manes and tails in summer and grow them back during the winter! This must be a handy trick of nature because without it, after a couple of years, their curls would turn into one big mess. The horses' winter coat is curled, but during summer it can almost be smooth. The winter coat can have light waves or strong curls, like a perm. Half of all foals get this curly coat, even if the Bashkir Curly is crossbred with a horse of a different breed.

Where do the horses come from?

There are different theories on the origin of the Bashkir Curly. After all, the three Bashkir Curlys that Peter Damele discovered did not fall out of the sky. Some people believe that the horse is a descendant of the Russian Bashkir pony, but there is no proof that ponies were shipped from Russia to the United States. Another theory is that the Vikings or Celts may have brought the horses, but there are no signs that there were horses in America after the Ice Age and before the Spaniards brought their horses to the continent. There are even more theories,
but they have all been rejected. Blood samples of the horses were taken to see if they belong to another breed, but these results were also inconclusive. Most likely, other breeds were involved, in particular the Quarter horse and the Morgan.

▼ Description

The present Bashkir Curly is a mid-size horse with a relatively small head, straight legs, strong knees, short back, round hindquarters and powerful shoulders. It has an exceptionally high number of red blood cells, and certain traits from primitive breeds. The hooves are almost perfectly round, strong and dark. The foals are born with a thick curly coat, curls in their ears and even curled eyelashes! They have a nice disposition and are intelligent horses.

Height
14.2 to 16 hands, usually around 15 hands.

Colors
The Bashkir Curly exists in all colors, as well as mixed and Appaloosa colored, but most horses are red chestnut.

▼ Use

The horses are very suitable for riding all disciplines in Western riding, reining, trail rides, jumping, dressage and endurance. They are very suitable for carriage driving.

▼ Gaits

In addition to the walk, trot and canter, some of the horses also know the foxtrot and the "running walk".

Many people with allergies seem to have a much less strong reaction to horses with a curly coat than to other horses!

Peruvian Paso Horse

In the 18th century, when roads were being constructed and horses and wagons were the norm, many people switched from breeding gaited horses to breeding trotting horses. The Peruvians however, kept on breeding their typical natural gaited horse, the Caballo Peruano de Paso. The Paso Peruano descends from the horses the Spaniards brought with them in the 15th century, which were blends between the Andalusian, the Barb, the Friesian and the Spanish Jennet horse. The Peruvians needed a horse they could use for work on the plantations, and at the same time could be a stable riding horse able to carry the rider from one place to the other, over steep mountains and sloping valleys.

Even though the Paso Peruano is an old breed in South America, it is still very recent in North America. It was imported only 30 years ago, but soon it had a mass of enthusiastic fans. This is probably not so strange because it is an extraordinarily elegant riding horse.

For more than a few hundred years the blood of other horses has been used when breeding this particular horse. It is the only breed in the world that can guarantee that 100 percent of the offspring will also have the characteristic natural gaits of the Paso Peruano.

▼ Description

The Paso Peruano should be muscular but still refined. The deep, expressive eyes make the horse look intelligent. The neck is more powerful than most light horse breeds, but is arched and elegant. Typical of this breed are the long manes, fetlock and the high-attached tail.

The Paso Peruano has something called brio. This is the natural energy and enthusiasm, which makes the horse look fiery. Even though it is a fiery breed, a lot of attention is paid to the character, which is why the Paso is friendly and easygoing. The breeders have consistently left out horses that did not have the correct temperament, even when they had great build. Many Paso owners say they have chosen it for it's exceptional good character.

Also termino is very typical for the breed: a flowing movement of the forelegs from the shoulder, which is almost like the arm motion of a swimmer. The foreleg is graciously brought

Height
14 to 15 hands.

Colors
Solid colors with dark skin are the most common: bay, black, buckskin, red, light gray, mouse, grulla, palomino and gray. Big white markings or a pinkish skin are not very desirable. Due to the direct Barb bloodline, these horses can have remarkable colors!

forward so that the hind leg can be put down calmly and without any problems in, or before the print of the foreleg. It is a unique movement, which makes it a pleasure to ride this horse.

▼ Use

The Paso Peruano is used as a riding horse.

▼ Gaits

The Peruvian Paso has classic gaits in four tempi, from a slow gait to quicker foot fall with the extended trot or collected canter. These natural gaits make the Paso a particularly fun riding horse.

Paso Llano – A slow, supple gait.

Sobreandando – A faster, long gait with staccato rhythm, which makes you out of breath.

There are about 12,000 Pasos in North America, and less than 20,000 in the whole world!

Paso Fino Horse

Like most horses that descend from Spanish horses, the Paso Fino is an extraordinarily elegant horse with a proud composure. The breed was created from the Spanish horses that came to South America about 500 years ago and they descend from the Barb, the Andalusian and the Spanish and Jennet horse. It is assumed that the breed also has blood from the Narraganset Pacer. In the United States, this is a very new breed. Breeding only began in the 1940's. The last couple of years, the breed has become very popular, and since 1992 the breed association has even grown by 60 percent.

At present there are more than 250,000 Paso Finos worldwide.

▼ Description

The Paso Fino is an incredibly beautiful horse, gracious but still energetic. The head is fine and elegant, the manes and tail are long and silky smooth. It is somewhat compact, with a deep breast and broad ribs. The horse is super smooth, fast and sturdy on its legs, and the breed is known for its strong hooves. With normal riding, shoes are not even necessary.

▼ Use

The Paso Fino is very suitable for rides and a popular instruction horse. Exhibitions are held in which the horses run competitions in different gaits. The breed is so versatile that these horses can be used for many more tasks, like farm work, wagon driving or reining. Because it is such a pleasure to ride, it is often used for therapy riding and riding with the disabled.

Height
13.2 to 15.2 hands (usually around 14 hands).

Colors
The Paso Fino might not exist in all the colors of the rainbow, but it does exist in all equine colors: spotted, bay, black, sorrel, gray, palomino and buckskin.

▼ Gaits

The Paso Fino's most exceptional characteristic is the gait in four tempi after which it was named, the "paso fino". All Paso Finos are born with this gait. The gait is executed in three variants, with a different level of collection:

Classic Fino is a very collected gait, at which the horse almost dances on the spot, with rapid foot fall and beautiful unbroken rhythm. Even though it moves its legs very fast, it only goes forward slowly – not faster than a slow walk.

Paso Corto is about as fast as medium trot and a very comfortable gait for the horse. It is fast and effective and a horse in good shape can keep doing this for hours without getting tired. Also for the rider this is a very comfortable gait.

Paso Largo is the gait with the least amount of collection and the most speed, but it still feels supple to the rider.

Chincoteague Pony

The small, cute and friendly Chincoteague ponies (pronounced: sjinko-teek) live on the islands of Chincoteague and Assateague, just off the coast of Virginia and Maryland. According to legend, they descended from the 17 Arabians that came ashore after swimming from a Spanish ship that was shipwrecked near the coast of Virginia sometime during the 17th century. When they arrived on the islands, for their survival, they were forced to eat the coarse cordgrass that was growing in the swampy landscape, as well as other crops. The horses were small and hardened, and they became the breed that is now called the Chincoteague pony. It's a nice story, but unfortunately it is more likely that the ponies are descendants from horses that were transported to Assateague in the 18th century, because the owners tried to evade taxes and perhaps certain other laws!

Wherever they came from, today there are two groups of ponies: the Maryland herd and the Virginia herd. The Virginia herd consists of 130 ponies that live on the Assateague islands. They are owned by the Chincoteague Voluteer Fire Company. The Maryland herd has about 140 ponies and is owned by the National Park Service in Maryland. On the border between Maryland and Virginia is a fence on the island, that keeps the horses separated. Because the ponies live in a national park, the herds cannot have more than 150 animals – otherwise they would cause too much damage to the environment.

Since 1924, Chincoteague has had a very special method of keeping the horse population contained: each year in July, amid festivities, a Pony Swim is held. The Chincoteague Volunteer Fire Company chases the ponies away from the island when the tide is slack, through the canal to Virgina. There the ponies are caught and the foals are auctioned off, after which the stallions and mares swim back. The swim takes about ten minutes.

The herd in Maryland is also controlled, but in a slightly different way. For these ponies, a unique preventative method was developed. They are injected with a contraceptive vaccine that makes them sterile for a period of one year. They can have these vaccines once a year. The method has been in use for eight years and it has proven to be effective and without side-effects. In the U.S. and Canada there are Chincoteague ponies in private ownership. Around the mid 1980s, the ponies were entered in a registry and today the Chincoteague pony is considered a rare breed.

▼ Description

The Chincoteague pony has great conformation, is strong and muscular and its tail and manes are very thick. It has a friendly character, is intelligent and versatile. It is a tough horse – it needs only some fresh water, seaweed, hay and some oats. In the winter it gets a thick coat and looks very cuddly.

Height
Up to 14 hands
(on average
12 to 13 hands).

Colors
Most ponies are spotted, with brown or yellow spots on a white coat. There are also ponies with solid colors, mostly black or chestnut.

▼ Use

The ponies on Chincoteague and Assateague live in the wild, which means they are not used for anything, but the ponies who are private property are used for riding.

The Chincoteague ponies drink twice as much water as other horses because of the high quantity of salt in their food. Because of these quantities of salt, they sometimes look fat and bloated!

It is sometimes claimed that the Chincoteague pony is so tough that during winter it only needs a bag of cement to lay on!

Some foals which were raised away from the island and received extra high-protein feed, grew to be just as big as regular horses!

Pony of the Americas

The Pony of the Americas (POA) was "born" in Iowa in 1954. One of the breeders of Shetland ponies, Les Boomhowers, had neighbors with an Arabian/Appaloosa mare that was pregnant by a Shetland pony. Les sold the foal, and the young stallion was white with scattered black spots, as if someone had poured a bucket of paint over him. Les immediately fell in love with him, especially because one of the spots on its hindquarters looked like a black hand print! The stallion was named Black Hand, and Les started dreaming of a new pony breed. He convinced several other breeders to believe in the dream, and a new pony breed was created. It needed to be a good pony for kids and youngsters, but also beautiful, fast and possess a good degree of stamina. It needed to have the head of an Arabian, the powerful body of a Quarter and the color of an Appaloosa! To create this horse the breeders had to use many horses and ponies during breeding: Arabians, English Thoroughbreds, Quarters, Appaloosas, Welsh ponies and Shetland ponies. The POA's popularity increased and in 1995, more than 45,000 ponies were registered.

▼ Description

The POA has an elegant, Arabian-like head, expressive eyes and refined ears. It is a strong, fast pony with a good deal of stamina, which looks more like a small horse than a typical pony. The eyes have a sclera: the iris of the eye is encircled with white, like with human eyes.

▼ Use

Very suitable for all kinds of riding. The POA is fast and strong enough for jumping and reining, and is patient and intelligent for dressage and instruction.

Height
11.2 to 13.2 hands.

Colors
Most POA's are Appaloosa-colored, usually with white on the loins and hindquarters and dark, oval spots. The patterns differ enormously. Some ponies have large spots everywhere, others are spotted. White spots on a dark coat is also possible. Around the nostrils, the POA has muzzled skin. The hooves are striped with vertical black and white stripes. There are also grays, but Paint and Pinto patterns are not allowed.

American Miniature

The Miniature horse is a "height breed". This means that horses of different breeds are registered, as long as they are under a certain height. A foal cannot be more than 30 inches tall, a yearling has to be under 32 inches, a 2-year-old horse cannot measure more than 33 inches and an adult horse cannot be higher than 34 inches. They have to be miniatures of big horses, and can look like Arabians, Quarters, Thoroughbreds and even pulling horses.

No dwarfs
The Miniatures are neither "genetic errors" nor dwarf versions of regular breeds. They have been deliberately bred to get a miniature horse, which looks like a regular horse – only smaller.

Use
The Miniatures are so small that only very small children can ride them. They are mainly kept as pets, almost like dogs. Exhibitions are organized with them and they have proven to be very suitable in therapy for disabled children and adults.

Transported easily
Miniature horses are easy to transport, you can just put them in the back of your station wagon. Just like dogs, they can also be transported on airplanes.

Pinto

The Pinto color probably comes from the Arabians that were shipped to America. Many believe that Pinto is the same as Paint, which is incorrect, even though the colors are the same. The American Paint Horse Association only has Painthorses, Quarterhorses and Thoroughbreds in their register, while the American Pinto Horse Association also registers miniature horses, ponies and horses of other breeds, like the Arabian, Morgan, Saddlebred and the Tennessee Walking Horse. The Pinto register has more than 107,000 entries.

If a spotted horse wants to qualify for the Pinto register, it has to have a minimum of 15 square inches of pink skin, with white hair on the body or certain designated places on the head if it is older than two years old. For yearlings, this should be 8 square inches and for foals 4 square inches. Ponies should have half of the surface and miniatures a quarter.

All horses can be registered, except Appaloosas and pulling horses. Pony stallions and miniature stallions should at least have one parent of a registered breed, whereas mares and geldings can always be registered if they have the right color.

▼ Pintos are divided into four categories:

Stock type – horses suitable for Western riding, terrain riding and many other competitions.
They should have the conformation of a Quarter horse.
Hunter type – suitable for terrain riding, Western riding and different disciplines.
They should have more of the conformation of the English Thoroughbred or a halfbred.
Pleasure type – suitable for Western riding, English riding and driving. The horses should be of the Arabian or Morgan type.
Saddle type – suitable for Western riding, English riding and wagon driving.
They should have the conformation of the American Saddlebred, Tennessee Walking Horse or Missouri Fox Trotter.

▼ Colors

The Pinto has two patterns: tobiano and overo.

A tobiano is white with large, colored spots, but the spots can be so large that it makes the horse look mainly colored. The spots are mostly on the head, breast, flank and hindquarters. The middle of the back is generally white.

The overo is a colored horse with white marks, mostly on its side. The marks are everywhere on its belly and spread out to the neck, hindquarters and legs. From the side, it looks as if the colors have been applied to the white. The face is often very white and some overos have white legs.

Palomino

Ever since Spanish horses set their hooves on American soil there have been Palomino colored horses. These beautiful, light gold animals with their white manes and tail were popular in Spain and were the absolute favorites of Queen Isabella of Bourbon. She had over one hundred in her stables, and only members of the royal house, or people with special permission, could ride them. The Palomino color is also called isabel, named after the queen. The color can be found in other breeds, but the horses of the queen were almost their own breed.

The American Dick Halliday created a Palomino register in the U.S. in 1935. The very first registered horse was the stallion El Rey de Los Reyes. Halliday has done many years of research on these horses, and has written many articles on them. In 1936 the register was renamed The Palomino Horse Association. All Palomino colored horses can be entered, no matter the breed, as long as they are between 14 hands to 17 hands. During the last years, cream colored horses with blue eyes have been allowed to register, because their descendants always seem to be Palomino colored.

▼ Color

The ideal Palomino color looks like a gold coin, but it can vary from gold-yellow to gold-brown. The manes and tail should be white, ivory or silvery, but 15 percent of darker or red hairs is allowed. The eyes are usually black or brown, and the skin is mostly gray, black or brown.